Mindful thoughts for
SURFERS

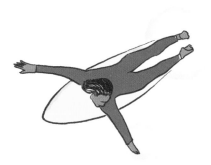

First published in the UK in 2020 by

Leaping Hare Press

An imprint of The Quarto Group
The Old Brewery, 6 Blundell Street
London N7 9BH, United Kingdom
T (0)20 7700 6700
www.QuartoKnows.com

British Library Cataloguing-in-Publication Data
A catalogue record for this book is available from the British Library

ISBN: 978-1-78240-895-6

This book was conceived, designed and produced by

Leaping Hare Press

58 West Street, Brighton BN1 2RA, UK

Publisher: *David Breuer*
Editorial Director: *Tom Kitch*
Art Director: *James Lawrence*
Commissioning Editor: *Monica Perdoni*
Project Editor: *Elizabeth Clinton*
Illustrator: *Lehel Kovacs*

Printed in China

1 3 5 7 9 10 8 6 4 2

Mindful thoughts for
SURFERS

Tuning in to the tides

Sam Bleakley

Leaping Hare Press

Contents

Blue Mindfulness

Wrapped in a cloak of seawater, surfing can take you out of your comfort zone, immersing you in a liquid environment. You become one with sealife. And as a temporary visitor, you must blend in.

The sea is a sensual world of beauty and brilliance, and if we can learn a deeper gratitude for the hospitality it offers, then we will deepen our own mindful states as we become ever more immersed in its wonders. If mindfulness is best described as bringing your attention to the moment and holding it fully, then joining the family of sea creatures, if only for a short while, is a remarkable way to achieve this state of being.

As surfers, our medium for mindfulness is the roiling, unfurling, shore-bound wave, an energetic shedding of the sea's skin that we attempt to ride with style. Surfing is a contour-fitting act, making best use of the wave's shape, speed and character – one of the purest thrills anyone can enjoy and one of the closest embraces of the natural world.

Tense and uncertain when you first learn, surfing becomes elastic and effortless as you gain experience. And as your confidence grows, so your intimacy with water grows. Surfing gets you inside the folds of the world, into the beating heart of its mysteries. The 'stoke' – used to describe the joy of riding waves – is the paradoxical and simultaneous balance of concentration and letting go, mixed together in a 'blue mindfulness'.

This 'blue mindfulness' may be a little different to the mindfulness of inner contemplation. What surfing teaches is that mindfulness is not 'in' you, but in the world of experience. Indeed, blue mindfulness is a letting go of inward contemplation as you embrace nature's expressions – salt showers, rainbows, moments when the ocean's skin folds over you, turning from navy to sapphire. Then, as you slot into your first tuberide, the sea reveals its secrets.

Surfing is a letting go of the desire to control and to know. In the letting go you are allowing the environment to take hold, to caress and to shape you. This is not always fun. Yet, as you bounce off the rocky reef, as you negotiate rip currents that want to drag you out to the horizon and as you brave the body-bending, mind-stretching lessons of the wipeout, to your surprise you find illumination in each encounter.

Then the coin flips and there is beauty; surfing with dolphins (scary too as they are big and unpredictable); standing tall at the tip of the longboard during your first noseride; riding all the way to shore where the sand bottom kisses you on arrival. Blue mindfulness is the enthusiastic embrace of these experiences in the present. A rinsing of the senses. A rinsing that is unforgettable and irresistible.

Sea-
awareness

While meditation might improve your surfing, surfing will definitely improve your surfing. But surfing can also be turned from mere activity into a meditation based on the sea's self-presentation – its patterns, moods and mysteries. Inward self-awareness ('ego-logy') becomes sensually embedded sea-awareness ('eco-logy').

The waves shave off personal pride, set by set. Let's take an example. A cluster of waves is forming on the horizon. Where will you paddle? As the set looms closer, you suddenly realize that the waves are much larger than you thought and breaking much further out. You paddle like crazy to get over the first wave, but get caught by the second wave that tumbles you underwater, and, as you burst up to break the surface for air, a third (and by far the biggest) wave hits you right on the head. We talk about being taken through the 'rinse cycle' as you are forced underwater, cartwheeled in the turbulence. After the fourth (smaller) wave puts you through another rinse, you emerge somewhat wiser.

Now you can position yourself for the next set, and now you know that the best wave to catch at this stage of tide, on this day, in this swell is probably the third in the four-wave set. Books do not teach you this. Immersive experience does. Sensually tuned immersive experience notches up the quality of awareness – a sea-awareness rather than a self-awareness. Once again, the mindfulness is not in the mind, but in the total ecology of the moment.

We could say that your positioning in the aforementioned example showed an initial lack of mindfulness. Or, you fell prey to hubris or conceit, thinking that you could outwit the ocean. Certainly, you did not quite read the script first time around. Again, the mindfulness is surely not in your judgement, but rather in the way that the environment attuned you or taught you how to better position yourself for the next set of waves. This is affordance – the sea affords or gives off a whole set of cues that shape your response. Mindfulness is, then, your entanglement with the sea as an 'attitude'.

Attitude literally means 'fitness' or 'posture'. So, mindfulness in surfing is a matter of how well you allow the sea's presence to shape your posture. Blue mindfulness is the fit between you, your board, and the contours of the waves that you surf. It is less a state of mind or being than it is a 'fitness' to surf; a best fit between what the sea affords (shape, sound and movement of the approaching set) and how you respond. Surfing as mindfulness is outside in.

The next cycle of sea-awareness begins as you paddle for that sizzling third wave (in the next set), rising with it, feeling it propel you forward as you spring to your feet. Every wave is different. The wave, not you, dictates whether you turn to the left or to the right. Think otherwise and you will be unceremoniously dumped. Again, being in tune is letting the shape of the wave shape your response. Can you afford not to notice that mindfulness in surfing is outside-in? The 'mind' in mindful surfing is a co-creation. What shape is the wave? Can you echo the wave's insistence – its prime quality – as you take off to ride to shore in this divine entanglement?

ACTIVE IMAGINATION

It may be better to compare this mode of mindfulness in surfing with active imagination, with dreaming and myth rather than traditional forms of meditation. The dream shapes you – you do not shape the dream. Myth forms us as it forms whole cultures. The imagination ventures forth and does or does not include 'you' – it becomes a mind of its own, independent, wilful and energetic.

'Let's go surfing' is not an act of will; it is a response to the call of the wild, where you do not sit and meditate but absorb the wild around you, learning from the ever-changing presentations of the coast, its shaping weathers and underwater contours that give personality to waves and, in turn, influence your personality.

'Soul surfing' or 'mindful surfing' eschews heroes and bullies. Surfing is an act of the social imagination that embraces not only other surfers but also the morphing head of the sandbar, the bobbing seal, the fish-skewering gannet, the pulsing bell of the jellyfish, and the tangle of seaweed exposed at low tide.

Attention to
Connection

Contrary to the aim of mindfulness as inner
contemplation, blue mindfulness is an emptying out
of oneself to achieve identification with the ocean.
It is a mindfulness that mirrors the ocean's expressions
of ever-changing surface turbulence and deep unseen
currents. These expressions can be compared to the
twin capacities of vigilant and paradoxical attention.

You wait patiently for a wave, like a seabird ready
to penetrate the oily skin of the sea. You can identify
with the seabird through your vigilant attention – a
constant round of watching and then acting – as the
bird plunges underwater and reappears a moment later
with a wriggling fish in its silver beak. At the same time

you are exerting a deep scan, taking in the background colours and textures of the sea; the fragrance of salt-laden air within which you are cocooned, all through paradoxical attention.

The wave approaches and unfurls and you catch it, take off, turn the board the way that the wave is breaking in one smooth action. You hug this mobile saltwater skin as it tells its moment-to-moment story in bursts of energy dissipation. You grasp the here and now as you comprehend the faraway. You are blue mindfulness, immersed in the joy of waveriding with both a focused and a scanning, appreciative attention.

THE STRING OF TIME

Surfboards traditionally have a backbone, called the 'stringer', running the entire length of the board from nose to tail. Within the world of surfboard design the shaped core gives the board buoyancy, the fin gives directional stability, and the stringer gives strength and flexibility. Most surfboard stringers are made of strips (one, two or three) of balsa wood either running vertically through the board or around its rail edges.

Balsa is a great wood for surfboard stringers: it is light, strong and flexible. In fact, the fast-growing balsa tree is a good teacher of attention. It grows 5 metres (16 feet) a year, reaching full height in six years. In balsa tree years, we can imagine a six-year-old tree as a 100-year-old person. But there is a big difference. The balsa tree has no annual growth rings, no visible memory within its substance. As people age, the year-on-year build-up of experiences can bring 'memory overload' to our minds. So many things happen that, if we do not give attention to accepting and resolving our experiences, we can lose the here and now. A balsa stringer is part of the board's thinking and expression, a key component of its personality. With its help we can get back to our own 'now'.

The board flexes through a surf session while maintaining core strength – with a mind of its own, you follow its motions and trajectories. In longboarding, the key skill is cross-stepping to the nose and the stringer supplies the directional track. As we attempt clean footwork, superb balance, excellent timing and effortless entry into and exit from a wave, we approach the cherished ideal of purity in surfing, where all the components of a ride lock in smoothly. But this would fail without the anchor of ever-pulsing background paradoxical attention, a constant act of noticing that is akin to the surfboard stringer – a backbone keeping us upright. The exercise of paradoxical attention is, simply, an identification with the ever-changing ocean. Where vigilant attention is force, paradoxical attention is presence.

As surfers, we are then part of the attention span of a networked world and varieties of environments both natural and human-made. We are present in this web of attention, where key objects or artefacts, such as the stringer, vibrate the web making differing calls upon us. And the surfboard is our primary link with the secrets of saltwater.

THREE MOVING SURFACES

The beauty of surfing is that it connects three moving surfaces – wave, board and the soles of your feet (if you stand – those with physical challenges may require seated or prone positions). Think about it. You only have a small surface area of your body in contact with a moving board in contact with a moving wave as part of a moving sea. All that water energy is transmitted up through the soles of your feet.

When riding a wave the 200,000 nerve endings in the soles of your feet are constantly being massaged by the board's surface on a highly unpredictable skin of blue-green-white water. Here, mindfulness is in the point of exchange between skin, moving plane and unfolding wave. Body, board and wave energy interweave. Once embedded in this attention to connection, the sea's calling will be stronger than ever as you navigate the ride – not by imposing your will on a wave, but responding to it in an artful balancing of vigilant and paradoxical attention.

Blessings
of the
Board

Surfing raises deep passions – about not only the quality of waves, but also the vehicles that allow us to ride these waves. Surfboards, extensively varied in design, are fetish objects over which much hot air is expressed as we test the merits of differing shapes, sizes and materials.

That a surfboard has a 'nose' and 'tail' already indicates that this item is treated like an animal – somewhere between fish and bird – alive and pulsing, sometimes tamed like a pet and sometimes wild and out of control, biting back.

We talk of 'shaping' surfboards (crafted by individuals or manufactured by machine), but surfboards also 'shape' the surfer. Being mindful in surfing means embracing the surfboard as a material extension of the person, an addition to and expression of character. Here, mindfulness in relation to the board extends to environmental awareness, where the surfer is drawn to renewable and non-polluting materials such as balsa, bamboo and paulownia wood. But beyond their environmental qualities and physical properties of strength and flexibility (long-cherished totems of surfboard performance), these fast-growing woods also play a spiritual role, bringing their blessings to the life of the board.

BAMBOO MUDRA

There is a story of a great ruler in India who set out to meet the Buddha, who was travelling with a retinue of monks. The ruler left home to dwell in a bamboo grove, knowing that the Buddha would pass through

the grove. Sure enough, the Buddha arrived. A crowd
had already gathered. They were curious not about the
Buddha, who they did not know, but about their ruler's
strange behaviour in retreating to the bamboo grove.
When the ruler prostrated before the Buddha and
asked for guidance, the crowd was shocked; they
thought the travelling retinue should be prostrating
themselves before the great ruler. But soon they saw
that the Buddha dispensed love and wisdom and
understood the meaning of their ruler's behaviour.

The two talked day and night and the ruler persuaded
the Buddha to stay and teach. The ruler gave the Buddha
the bamboo grove, and there the Buddha set up camp
with the monks and taught the local community. In
time, the ruler died, the Buddha died, and the community
moved on. Meanwhile, the bamboo grove grew in size
and splendour, the canes swaying in the breeze.

Imagine if the bamboo used to make surfboards
had a lineage that reached back to that ancient grove.
Bamboo has a memory, a morphogenetic imprint of

every event that ever happened in its grove. Every board made with this bamboo would then be, in a sense, a living Buddha. Every surfer who rides such a board would be riding with the Buddha's imprint, the board shaping the rider's responses and the board's responses in turn rooted in the wave's unfolding.

Mindfulness is not in the 'mind' of the surfer, it is in the relationship between the surfer and the board, which is a sliver of unbroken memory, a splinter of unfolding time within the eternal unspooling wave forms of nature. Within all this commotion – all this motion and sound – there is calm, stillness and silence; within all this change there is permanence.

TUBERIDE TO THE BODYMIND

If the Buddha were amongst us today, would they be a surfer? If they were of the Zen school (imagine: the Buddha having to pick a school of thought!) would their bliss be total immersion in the tuberide – aquamarine wall curling over, jade-green exit framed as pure symmetry, all noise cancelled, time elastic, the final sensory explosion as you are spat out amid compressed air, the last exhalation of the breaking wave?

The Buddha might agree that the mindful moment here is not in you but in the blue body of nature that surrounds you, alongside which and in concert with, you are inhaling and exhaling, emerging rinsed and renewed. You are housed by the moment, the mindful wrap, which you can learn to receive, with grace, as the greatest gift and the deepest meditation.

The Buddha might also identify so closely with the experience of the tuberide that separating out its individual parts – including the human ego – would serve no purpose. Surfing, in this sense, is bodymindful. This is a state of tuning inside-out to the surrounding environment rather than tuning outside-in to your mind.

A Place
Together

Surfing is not all go-it-alone, but is usually a social activity where entanglement and enmeshing are inevitable. Of course, a lot of surfers crave an uncrowded break and talk of sessions where 'no one was out' and 'I had it all to myself'. But surfing is never solitary if your mindset is one of connection. You are always surfing within the great bodymind of the ocean, a living environment made up of many components that wash around you, move with you and swim beneath you. And your surfboard is an extension of your own bodymind.

Surfing with others intensifies the need for a social outlook, and surfing with crowds brings this collaborative consciousness to a peak. Crowd surfing will become increasingly common as waveriding continues to grow in popularity. Doing this gracefully and with equanimity demands reciprocity, supreme awareness and tolerance.

CROWD SURFING

A mindful approach to surfing in crowds is one of helpful sharing. Surfers should not be greedy. If you keep a cool head, support those lower down the pecking order of ability and agility, then everyone will get their fair share of waves. Sharing is not easy when we grow up in competitive rather than collaborative climates. But sharing is one of the first lessons kids have to learn. For some surfers, feeding off the energy of a crowd can be exhilarating. When the sea is crowded try to immerse yourself fully in the moment. A mindless immersion in a crowd jangles the nerves, leading to resentment. A mindful immersion in a crowd demands generosity and hospitality.

The ancient Greeks did not surf, but as surfers we can be inspired by their placing of hospitality at the top of a hierarchy of social musts. Hospitality at sea, particularly in your backyard, at your local beach, is an important aspect of mindful surfing. Why be a hostile local? The sea is not your property. It is part of our shared planet. Your energy will just dissipate if you worry about territory and ownership. Relax.

The bigger beat in any surf session is the rhythm of sets and lulls that the sea reveals and conceals. Tune in to this rather than being niggled by a crowd. Those more attuned to this pattern might find space in the crowd. What would the surfing Buddha do in a surfing crowd? Maybe they would attract kudos by emanating a cool-headed calmness amongst chaos, setting the tone of collaboration and hospitality with a deep presence.

The best way to stand out from the crowd is to immerse yourself in it.

THE STILL POINT OF BALANCE

Waves come in sets and dolphins in pods. They are communities. Dolphins work in teams to create underwater vortices that help to propel a single dolphin in their leap out of the water. The poise and control in this dolphin-leap moment is a bit like the still point of balance in surfing, where the downward force of gravity (from your body position) and the upward force of buoyancy (from your board position) are in line, keeping things stable, even through fast, sometimes airborne, movement. This rule of balance is essential to a successful ride inside the tube, where time seems to expand and happen in slow motion. Some might never experience that moment in a tube, but we can still turn other aspects of surfing into meaningful experiences.

We can discover that still point of balance elsewhere; perhaps everywhere. You may get caught by a thunderous set and be humiliated. But this can be flipped from a negative into a positive. Allow the luminous white cauldron of foam to bounce you to shore, laughing out loud, then paddle out in the next lull using the deeper-water channel where the waves do not break. Sit up and enjoy the view, bathed in reflected light.

Think: was I just shown the still point of balance inside that furious cauldron?

Surfing is a celebration of place, not just a riding of waves. Enjoy the energy and movement of the sea around you. Enjoy the crowds, recognizing all joy and pain, all successes and failures as your own. Engage with rips and currents. Know the fluidity and surprise of sets coming and going, the shorebreak pounding, the incessant tidal layers, without the necessity of catching a wave. Celebrate this surf-less surfing. Almost certainly, especially when the surf is poor – on a bleak, windy onshore day – a fellow surfer will tell you 'it's rubbish'. Tell them that you deliberately did not catch a wave, but you had a great surf.

When you walk up the beach, surfing goes on without you. Someone, somewhere, is always on a wave. In the blue mindfulness that belongs to all surfers, and none, you are in a place together, always surfing with the great mind of the ocean.

Saltwater
Play

The energy and excitement kids bring to surfing is infectious. Even if a successful ride lasts only seconds, those moments are etched upon kids' faces. They exemplify the Buddhist idea of the 'beginners mind' – uncluttered, without prejudice, open. If we pay attention, kids will teach us as much as we teach them. And through slowing down to play we can seize the opportunity to discover mindfulness. We cannot be children again, but we can learn to leave our (often illusory) burdens and preoccupations on the shore and rediscover our playful spirit in the company of those for whom spontaneity, imagination and delight are the only things that matter.

It's no surprise that water calls to kids. Adult bodies are 50–65 per cent, while infant bodies are 75–78 per cent water. Before birth, we were all suspended in amniotic fluid, swimming in the womb for nine months. We are nascent bodysurfers, even if our first ocean is compact. So, when a baby is born in a water bath, they will naturally hold their breath. This is called the infant diving reflex – when in water, breathing ceases, the heart rate slows automatically and the eyes open – lasting until six months of age. It is strange that, as we grow into children, we have to learn to swim again.

KIDS IN THE CURL

Many kids will start out frightened of waves, which is quite natural. So, it's important to deal with this fear gently. It can take a long time to gain confidence and proficiency in the surf, so you have to make sure that children enjoy the process. Saltwater play goes hand-in-hand with saltwater safety – choosing sensible equipment and entering waves that suit a child's skill and confidence level to make sure they don't feel intimidated. But also, we should 'scaffold' learning. Taking the time to allow kids to feel fully safe at the stage they are at establishes the solid confidence upon which we build upwards into new skills and newer, riskier (and more exciting) thrills.

A great motivator is seeing other more experienced kids venturing further out, perhaps inspiring the less adventurous to join them in deeper waters. Outback, sitting in the line-up can give kids, and adults, a sense of pride as they identify with the surfing community. To say 'I am a surfer', whatever challenges you face, is to have worth and a sense of belonging.

A CHANGE OF FOCUS

Riding waves provides a magical window of opportunity for anyone suffering from anxiety. Kids experience anxiety as much as adults do and being in water can provide a safety valve for their emotions. And it is available to everyone. The feel of saltwater on your skin; the charged ions of turbulent water; your active body learning to dance on the wave face (releasing all those pleasure chemicals) – all take you into a world of connection and shared play. Here, we shift away from whatever the mind was focused on that had us stuck or anxiously preoccupied.

It's a good idea to invite and embody playful learning. A competitive approach drilled in turns surfing into a chore. Let natural ability emerge at its own pace. Allow a child to explore their senses – something you can do as an adult, too. At the water's edge, come to the present moment – look at the colour, texture and movement of the sea. Feel the wind, smell the seaweed, taste the salt, hear the waves raking sand, work that sand through your toes. Make up a fun rhyme about the things around you and sing it as you wade in, laughing out loud. Just don't laugh underwater!

Sensations can be relished: the strength of the current, the warmer shallow sections, water on the face. Stay at waist depth while tuning in to the pace and power of the whitewater. As you turn to catch it, the foam will have a joke with you and, like a bucking seahorse, might throw you off. But you won't get hurt. Picture someone whispering 'relax' into your ear. Take a pause before you pop up. Then you'll spring to your feet instinctively.

Surfing's curriculum is wide – getting to know the ocean and sealife, sharing waves with playmates. Explore the living classroom of rock pools. Scurry with crabs, flit like shrimps or wait for the tide to turn like limpets. Between rides, pretend you're sealife, bursting out of the water and plunging below.

Learning
from the
Wipeout

The wipeout is not just a physical process of falling off during a ride. It is also an emotional process of facing up to the fact that, at that point, the wave's bundled energy, saltwater passion and rapid motion outwitted you. A wipeout signals that you are not perfect. Wipeouts quickly strip away the ego and, if you let them, build character. Learning from experience is a prime tenet of mindfulness. And the underwater rinse cycle feeds right into muscle memory and exercises the questioning mind. The wipeout is a pathway to humility.

An ungainly somersault within the turbulent coil of the wipeout can paradoxically offer both a sensual and spiritual experience – as if you are reborn from the belly of the whale (sometimes with a bulging sinus infection). If you surrender to the moment you'll notice how the wave pressure creates a perfect underwater cylinder. Inside this you might hear an eerie noise like a low growl of a hungry animal combined with a keening, sinister wail.

Tales from hunting societies, such as the Inuits, tell of their shaman's ritual descent to the underworld. Before the hunting season begins, the shaman 'dies' on behalf of the community, meets with the animal soul – the totem of the tribe – asks forgiveness for hunting and then is 'reborn'. After resurfacing from heavy wipeouts, you may feel as though you've undergone a similar journey. The kernel of your self-imposed terror is a huge adrenaline rush to which big wave riders, in particular, become addicted. The wipeout can be a near-death experience. For most, it is a simple reminder that, in attempting to master the waves, the sea will always master you, tumble and humble you.

THE BIGGER BEAT OF NATURE

As your surfing improves, your wipeout frequency will definitely decrease, but your wipeout intensity will increase as you place yourself in gradually more radical conditions. This might smack of heroism and a need for victory at sea (as if one day you'll be a big wave-riding titan). So, another way to approach the wipeout is to frame it as a learning experience – a part of surfing to be embraced. If we accept that wipeouts are inevitable, we will see them not as errors but as punctuation marks in the sentences and texts we inscribe on the surf.

Rather than avoiding the wipeout, take risks, ride on the edge and let the lip clip you from time to time. Roll with it, sacrificing yourself to the shamanic sea-belly of the whale and the bigger beat of nature. After all, you probably won't lose your board because you will be using a leash.

The leash stretches under tremendous pressure, but then relaxes back to its original length. In some ways the leash is a metaphor for the body rinsed by mindful awareness in a wipeout, stretched and tumbled, gradually recovering its original shape and orientation, but now with this shamanic experience stitched into its fabric. And so, the bodymind is stretched to its limit before returning to itself with a difference; with new sense drawn from a fast tubing wave and a quick trip over the falls.

RISK-TAKING

Applying mindfulness to an activity not only turns an event into an experience that offers authentic learning, it also 'scaffolds' learning by supporting risk-taking or imaginative leaps beyond current capability into future expertise. One foot is firmly planted in the known, and the other, leading foot, is reaching out into the unknown, through a step-wise adventure into new terrain.

Some surfers (often longboarders who can cross-step up-and-down their board) will abandon the leash, forcing themselves into a more vulnerable situation where the wipeout is a constant 'ghost' companion. But they have also learned how to grab the board as they fall to stop it darting to shore or hitting others.

Part of mindful surfing is always to project your imagination into future possibility, carefully testing your limits. This requires peripheral attention – a grasp of context known as 'paradoxical attention'. Paradoxical or free-floating attention is long span, while vigilant or focused attention is short span (noticing only what is right under your nose).

An imagination that can stretch into the future, but which is also tethered in the reality of what is known, lives in the realm of the real and the possible, forging a grounded identity. Mindful surfing embraces the paradox of 'surf safe but always push your limits'. Unleash your potential but leash your hubris. A loose board signals loose attention.

Power
of the Pod

Surfing with dolphins is unforgettable; watching them leap, especially. Dolphins in pods leap so high because they work collaboratively to produce strong vortices and eddies in the water that supplement muscle power and allow the lucky individual to burst higher and further. What better model for movement through water than a pod of dolphins? Surfboards extend the human body to become a little like dolphins, enabling glide and arc, but also zippy, fast turning.

The secret to surfboard design is to 'think' with the board – its material components and its shape. The material world offers us the opportunity to expand our consciousness. Unskilful design results in a cumbersome, dull life full of unwanted junk. Skilful design enhances life through beauty and an aesthetic of timeless expression. The Greek root of 'aesthetic' means 'sense impression' and aesthetics expand our senses.

The design of the surfboard, which extends our body, expands our sense of bodily awareness in the water, helping us to become more animal-like. This means better surfing; mindful surfing that treats the surfboard as a living animal companion, not the dead weight of inorganic matter. Mindfulness, in this equation, is neither transcending nor shedding matter, but embracing the material world of which we are extensions and creating beauty out of matter.

FROM FINLESS TO THRUSTER

For thousands of years people around the world have ridden waves on finless wooden boards fashioned from local trees. As surfing developed, the addition of fins allowed for change of direction with stability. Contemporary surfers who want to go back to the roots of waveriding continue to experiment with finless boards. They tend to skate all over the place, but once mastered, afford an unforgettable sensation of sliding. In contrast, surfboards with fins have traction, so the back end of the board does not slide, but glides.

Early boards, dating from the explosion of surfing in California in the 1950s, were over 2 metres (9 feet) long with large D-shaped fins commonly placed at the far tail. The most experimental of fins – or 'skegs' – was the tunnel fin, shaped so that it would hold water, making the back end of the board heavier, and thus easier to noseride from the front. The theory – not based on any animal model – was better than the practice and the design was soon abandoned. Most shapers and surfers agreed that the fin should model the hydrodynamics of sealife and be placed a little way up from the tail for better steering.

When boards went radically short in the mid-to-late 1960s, they were still single-finned. New long, raking and flexible fins were inspired by the dolphin's dorsal fin, allowing carving arcs and 'S' shaped turns. Surfing moved from straight lines to vertical manoeuvres and the use of a low centre of gravity.

Later, 'fin boxes' were invented – plastic slide-in boxes where fin placement could be adjusted, either closer or further away from the tail of the board according to preference. This transcended the fixed fin and gave surfers greater freedom to try different fin sizes and shapes, just as sea creatures possess a myriad of different designs – deeper fins for greater traction and sharper turning; shorter fins for a looser feel.

Take a look at your board. Ask yourself: do you know the origin of its design? How many different shapes have you tried before this one? Do you have a vital sense of the unbroken line stretching back, connecting this board to the first? Can you picture your board as a living agent, scion of history, memory, thought?

In the early 1980s three-finned shortboards dominated, designed around the same principle as dolphins collectively creating vortices of water for extra energy. The two side fins create turbulence around the central fin and this gives extra thrust to the board – hence these were called 'thrusters'. Prior to the development of the thruster, the 'twin fin' board gave an impressive speed boost but caused a lot of turbulence at the back. Surfers could now choose from the gift of stability from a central fin, or stability paired with the thrust from the side fins. And as longer, easier to ride boards were reintroduced, there was soon a shape available for every level of ability.

Biomimicry – design inspired by nature – is a key part of this refinement and recasting of surfboard performance. Surfers absorb the active vocabulary of sealife and translate it into waveriding. This pondering and interpretation is a central part of a deep and subtle mindfulness gained from surfing – an expression of an immersive, embodied vocabulary. The muscle and cartilage of the dolphin is converted into arc, torque and acceleration on the wave face, where fin imitates fin through the power of the pod.

Be Like
Water

In the Tao Te Ching, the Chinese sage Lao Tzu celebrates the qualities of water:

'It benefits all things without contention. In dwelling, it stays grounded. In being, it flows to depths. In expression, it is honest. In confrontation, it stays gentle. In governance, it does not control. In action, it aligns to timing. It is content with its nature and therefore cannot be faulted.'

Lao Tzu's observations, however, contain paradoxes. Water's range of expression includes the extremes of ice and steam. Is water really 'gentle' in confrontation? Try telling that to a big-wave surfer as a thirty-foot-high liquid bomb explodes in front of them!

'The supreme goodness' – the highest state of moral life – 'is like water,' says Lao Tzu. It is shape-shifting and adaptable; it absorbs as it expresses. The most destructive of human traits is the inability to absorb contrasting views.

Taoists do not look to metaphors of nature as instruction on how to live, but instead to direct instruction from nature. They believe we are a component of nature and nature is an expression of Tao. For example, if there is no motion in the direction you want to go from the place where you are (such as being caught inside a bigger breaking set while paddling out), find the place that you can go (catch the whitewater back to the beach) and that way you will keep going to the place you want to go (so that you can join the flowing water in the rip current and paddle back out in the deep-water channel). That is what water would do. If you choose the ocean as your teacher, then do not turn your back on it. Do what water asks; in other words, flow.

YIN & YANG

Non-surfers probably imagine that surfing is the ultimate go-it-alone activity, definitely not a team sport. But this is not strictly the case. The line-up can be hectic, chaotic and sometimes dangerous, causing surfers to come close to colliding. Yet, when the sea is crowded and the atmosphere agitated, do you notice the water complaining? No, it simply flows. Taoism advises us to be like water, to adapt and flow. But this is just a starting point.

Surfing is not about becoming like water; it is embarking on a different path of becoming because of water. Water is the medium of change, not the substance into which you will change as a surfer. Sometimes, water is not your friend. Even smaller waves, sculpted hollow by an offshore wind or a pebble seabed, can whip you 'over the falls' – no fun if they are smacking onto a sharp and poisonous coral reef. We can call these 'curtain razors', as they promise an inglorious end to your just-begun performance!

The Taoists generally say that water is yin – absorbing, adaptable. But that is for the brook, the stream and the flat sea. I see waves as more yang and 'tough'. They fight back. Then, water is relentless. It never stops. When restricted, it seeks the weakest spot of any obstruction and applies constant pressure until it is free. Water is opportunistic. Given the slightest opening, it will pass through. Water is a force as much as it is a presence.

Perhaps one way to read Taoism is as a philosophy of opportunism. Whichever way the flow goes, one follows. A famous Hawaiian surfboard brand called Town & Country uses the Taoist yin-yang symbol in black and white. Some surfers may not know about its origins in Taoism. In the 1970s and 80s Town & Country's groundbreaking test pilots were among the most futuristic surfers in the world. Balance through extreme motion was their trademark. They rode radical board shapes called 'stingers', which stimulated the senses (because they were so fast-turning) and made the rider hyper-alert. This kind of surfing inspired progressive skateboarders, who by the 1990s had re-inspired surfers, for whom getting airborne (the 'aerial') and then landing cleanly back on the wave was at the cutting edge of surfing.

At the very heart of their skills was a celebration of water as 'flow'. The interpenetration and balance of yin and yang in Taoism can only ever be apprehended in terms of temporary, shifting states; as the flow of energies into, against and through one other. This lesson of impermanence is deeply important for mindfulness and surfing. The more you think you can master water, the greater will be your disappointment. The more you roll with water, the better the ride.

Grommets
& Titans

Ever since modern surfing exploded in popularity in 1950s' California, kids who surf have been nicknamed 'grommets' or 'gremmies' (from 'gremlins': mischievous creatures in folklore). They are an essential part of the surfing community not just because they are its future, but also because they keep older surfers on their toes.

Grommets surf naturally, without affectation. Their perspective is always the present. Yet, out of the water, even the young are exposed to stress. The pressures of expectation (from peers or adults) or the worries taken on from parents who, perhaps, cannot make ends meet, can weigh heavily. In response, some countries have introduced mindfulness sessions in schools. If you are lucky enough to live near a coast with surf, what better medicine than to bring your complete attention to the flow of seawater and the thrill of attempting to ride a breaking wave to shore?

Surfing feels like child's play when you are absorbed but not overwhelmed. And if play is put hand-in-hand with safety, surfing is a positive experience for all. Surfing safely is, of course, best achieved when the surf is under waist height for small wave stoke. These are my favourite conditions to surf with my family. This is important in mid-winter (in temperate climates) when, despite modern wetsuits keeping you relatively warm, you still 'flush through' in a tumbling wipeout. These cold rinses (and their partner-in-crime, the sinus infection) are lessened if the waves are less fierce.

However, all of this wave height talk is from my adult perspective. The knee-to-waist wave for one person may be over-the-head to another. Mindful surfing should involve understanding the relative nature of heights and depths. Surfing teaches humility – it will bring you down a peg and show you where you stand in the relative scales of ability, experience, physical strength, preparedness, and so on. When you kick out of a small wave and say 'that was a breeze', think of the person who just surfed a similar wave behind you – to them it was a wild overhead grinder as they let out a joyous hoot flying past. Perhaps that was you not so long ago.

A TASTE FOR ADRENALINE

One day, perhaps, the elusive hundred-foot wave will be ridden (and recorded). But you can bet that legend will have had their fair share of life-threatening wipeouts. Yet it is true that most surfers don't crave big waves, preferring smooth, long, gently wind-combed peelers. Quality, not size or quantity.

But our future legend will have conquered the greatest source of panic within surfing – tackling those monsters. They will have learned how to hold their breath and stay calm in those long, tumbling descents into the underworld. In that black torrent, the biggest danger is disorientation; panic can set in because you are not sure whether you are swimming to the surface or the sea's carpet. At this point, big-wave specialists will often draw on relaxation and attention-focusing meditative techniques to pin them to the moment and to maximize calm attention, resulting in skilful (and potentially life-saving) action, not battling the turbulence, but letting it pass (sometimes for a full minute) before swimming up to the surface.

You might think that conquering big waves needs a big ego, but the best big-wave titans tend to be humble. They know that the waves will bring them low at every opportunity, and an inflated ego is your worst enemy. Leave the inflation to your flotation vest (in severe hold-downs, it will quickly bring you to the surface).

However, surfing slightly bigger and bigger waves is a great education. You realize the world around you is affording you experiences; you are not its shaper. Just at the point of balance on your biggest wave yet, you are cartwheeled at the sea's whim. Did 'spirit', in its aspiration to reach the heights, tip over into the trough of hubris? What will 'soul', plunging into depths of suffering, do with this humiliation? Will it rise into higher understanding? If you stay attached to mindful curiosity you can embrace the paradox of the peak and the trough, finding knowledge in unhooking yourself from a desire for one and aversion to the other.

If you are ambitious enough to hurtle down heavier wave faces, start safely. You were a grommet once. Perhaps, in some ways, you still are.

Small waves are great healers, safely channelling your energies, helping you towards better emotional health and supporting so many people who may struggle to find fulfilment or remedy elsewhere. Then, if you get a taste for adrenaline, go bigger. But don't let your head swell as the sea swells, upwards into monsters. Big waves are the great leveller.

Waves of
Freedom

You could say that, in one way or another, many of us have become unwitting captives to the habitual act or ritual of consumption that we now realize is destroying the planet for future generations.

Surfing too is subject to these darker forces – a culture of popular consumption has grown up around it, in which surf gear and fashion-based clothing are coveted, purchased and discarded in prodigious quantities. These can be polluting (nasty chemicals used in surfboard production) and exploitative (cheap labour).

Yet, out in the ocean with a clean swell running, a surfer can feel a sense of freedom kick in that seems unburdened by any contradiction between what is consumed and what is experienced from the board's privileged vantage point. Out there, you feel detached from the burden of society. But is this freedom, this contentment, grounded in mindfulness and *ahimsa* ('non-harm' – a key principle in Buddhism, Hinduism and Jainism)? Or is it a contentment that allows complacency to grow within it?

A famous advert for surfing apparel ran in magazines some time back. It said 'only a surfer knows the feeling', referring to that immense sense of liberation out in the ocean. This feeling of freedom is what characterizes mindful activity. But, if freedom is to become more than superficial – a mere surface current – we need to shift mindfulness from a cultivation of inner sense to one of a 'common' sense: a social mindfulness.

Social or extended mindfulness is based on ideals such as acceptance of difference, tolerance of others, kindness to all beings and care for our shared environment. The language for this concept comes from the world of finance: 'bonding', 'exchange', 'trust', 'security'. But perhaps we can repurpose these terms, and not merely as description. Rather, the language could be performed so that it creates social action – directly and as it is uttered – in which the capital of freedom that the surf affords is fairly distributed to all who access the sea.

Surfing requires acts of bonding with the coastal environment, exchanging with the surfing community, trusting in your equipment, and making secure (through practice and gaining confidence) your relationship with the unpredictable, unfolding wave. This is not an economic model, but the immediate reality of expressive water slapping your skin.

NATURAL CURRICULUM

Waves are great symbols for freedom of movement. They manifest through winds creating friction on the sea surface. That energy translates through water until this spreading circular movement 'feels the bottom' of coastlines, takes on shape and body (over rock or coral reefs, sand or cobble beaches, down headlands or points), rises up and breaks, releasing energy (articulated by physicists in a feast of equations, felt by surfers in the graceful swoop of a bottom turn).

The movements of the waves provide wonderful and intimate embodied metaphors for the kinds of freedom of movement that can be achieved in a social group whose common activity is 'taking off' to surf 'open faces' and 'kiss the lip', roll 'toes on the nose' or 'soul arch' through a section.

With this embodied experience of living well on the wave in our minds, can we carry it forwards – can we 'surf' life? Together, in every way? Can we yoke with others and act for the survival of our surfing sites and communities, our countries, our species and our planet?

Doing and fairly exchanging (skills, knowledge, equipment, labour) within the surf community is not just for sport or leisure. It runs much deeper. Commitment to the ideal of what was once called a 'soul surfer' – here a 'mindful surfer' – demands study of a 'natural curriculum'. This includes how to read wave shapes, reef passes, beach morphology, rip currents, tidal changes, wind formations, weather patterns and more. Surfers become lay geographers, geologists, oceanographers and biologists.

But we can push this natural curriculum further, into the realms of ethical action, ecological and emotional or spiritual awareness. Just as the surfing world has generated its own surfing lore, validated within the community of surfers, and just as surf culture produces lay academics adept at combining meteorology, topography and bathymetry (the study of underwater depths and ocean floors), so the surfing world can apply itself to developing truly sustainable forms of material consumption and future-proof, inclusive practices that have at their heart the intention to give everyone connected to surfing (however indirectly) a share in its freedoms equally and fully.

Tuning In
to the
Tides

The tides are the lungs of the ocean, rising and falling. An in-breath – the moon moves closer to the earth and pulls at the body of water, stretching its skin. An out-breath as the moon moves away – the skin of the ocean relaxes back and the tide subsides.

The tide is a timepiece. The word 'tide' comes from the old English and German words for 'time' (*tid* and *Zeit*). Tidal flow is an affordance of mindfulness. It locks us into rhythms. The word 'rhythm' comes from the ancient Greek root, meaning 'to flow' – and so we come back to water and the sea in all its restless states.

I have surfed all over the world, but I love witnessing in West Cornwall, UK, the large 7-metre (20-foot) tidal range – meeting a crescent of quartz and mica sand at high tide; the plain of rivulets and rock pools revealed at low tide. The smell of coconut and pineapple emanates from gorse blossom in spring and early summer, while once-rare choughs (birds that are the Cornish emblem) hover above the cliff sides. Adders might cross your path, looking for a place to sun themselves as you race down the cliff, board in tow, a swell running. Above, a kestrel eyes its prey.

With a grinding swell and a rising tide, the sea will race to deposit its entire weight on the beach in powerful pulses. This is particularly impressive during spring tides, where the sun and moon align and increase the gravitational pull on the ocean. The extra energy is tangible.

The combined effect of the moon and sun varies throughout the month. When moon and sun are in concert (at full moon and new moon) this produces the largest tidal ranges (spring tides). At so-called 'first quarter' and 'last quarter' the moon and sun work against each other, resulting in smaller tidal ranges (neap tides).

It is a remarkable phenomenon, two gravitational forces pulling at the elastic body of the world's oceans as they either join together or stand opposed. If it were strong enough, the Moon's gravitational pull would strip the Earth of its waters and scatter them into space. But, of course, the tides are by no means weak. They are a majestic force, and arguably the most reliable source of energy available.

Complementing this tidal flux are weather changes. Water evaporates from the seas and returns as rain. Big tides often come with dramatic weather shifts. The sea seems to suck in the sky's temper. A glowering sky, threatening rain or a thunderstorm, is absorbed into the sea and filters down.

Sitting there, in the swell, with lightning about to be thrown down, brings home how small the human figure is against the immensity of the ocean. These are times when surfing really reminds us how the body is transient, just a punctuation mark in the long narrative aeons of Earth.

DRINKING THE SEAS DRY

The tides are not to be tamed. In Norse mythology, Thor, god of thunder, is challenged to a drinking contest by the giant Utgarda-Loki. Thor drinks from his horn with gusto, but despite his best efforts, cannot drain it. He has been tricked; the giant has connected the horn to the oceans, so Thor is in fact trying to drink the seas dry. The giant mocked Thor for his weakness. But from then on, so the legend goes, the seas rose and fell as an echo of the valiant efforts of Thor to complete the impossible task.

Let's return to our lone surfer in the swell, set against the great backdrop of the shifting tides. Thor is rumbling thunder, the sudden flash of lightning, the immense charcoal cloud pregnant with rain. You might dream you are that mighty god, embodiment of immense strength. But Thor himself could not drink the seas dry, so no wonder that you feel anxious or moody – you will never master the weather, the overhanging cloud, the low brooding sky. You must, rather, become it. Wear the weather. You are sitting out there on a stormy swell, beaten by the rain. No wonder you feel insignificant. And then a cough from Thor and a huge curtain of water follows the push of the tide. You ride that wave until it collapses in a white heap on the beach and you inhale with the lungs of the tide, married to the moon's gravity.

No Pressure

Low-pressure weather systems, or depressions, are the source of the strong winds that blow across the oceans and seas, generating surf. So, as surfers, we like depressions and all their expressions.

On land and in everyday life, however, where a different kind of depression descends upon us, it's another story. In the place that American novelist William Styron called 'darkness visible', it is so easy to feel chronically low, anxious, heavy-hearted and miserable. For some, all sense of self dissolves and a big black hole opens up before them. Many turn to doctors, whose default treatment, more often than not, has been to prescribe antidepressants.

So many prescriptions have been given that, in some countries, traces of antidepressants are now present in the groundwater. But there is a recent and welcome trend to treat depression with alternatives to pharmaceuticals, including the 'green gym' (walking, running, cycling) and the 'blue gym' (swimming and water sports). When mindfulness is added to the equation, the results can be dramatic.

LIFETIME PRESCRIPTION TO THE BLUE GYM

In the playground of the blue gym, surfing as therapy is tried and tested. What better medicine than to paddle into a set and launch down the rain-slicked face of one of the best waves you ever tasted, salt stinging your eyes? A big, swooping bottom turn and you glance up – double overhead and looming, the fringe of the lip throwing out foam; finding a sweet spot, you hurtle back down faster than ever before, slice a clean cutback, readjust and kickout in the shorebreak.

As you spend time in breaking waves, there are increases in serotonin, oxytocin and dopamine levels – all good stuff for feeling in tune with the world. Surfing is also good for the heart, as both a love-like passion and heartbeat raiser. It exercises the big fist of muscle and its many connecting vessels, elevating adrenaline, tuning reflexes, and toning the mind to create calm and acceptance.

As you get active in the blue gym (and as you release all those endorphins), practising mindfulness brings added benefits. A growing body of evidence shows that learning mindfulness – defined as training the mind to focus on the present moment and to maintain attention, while also being aware of sensations and your immediate surroundings – can reduce anxiety.

This happens when the mind is encouraged to stop jumping ahead into thoughts about the future, or ruminating compulsively about the past to the extent that emotions like worry, fear and anger cloud the present. When morbid thoughts dominate, that cloud is filled with stories of our own making, and we lose connection with reality as it really is.

When we enter the blue gym and get moving, when we relax and get into activities that are simply fun, that are not about achieving anything – such as noticing the pulsing bell of a jellyfish or wiping out on a small wave – then we are on the path to mindful happiness and a life lived beyond the confines of our worry-cloud.

STORM TO STORM: MERGING & MELANCHOLY

Historically, 'depression' was seen differently than it is now. In western medieval and Renaissance societies, there was a personality type called the melancholic. This person was often isolated, but they were also seen as reflective and intellectual. Melancholia was thought of as grey and leaden, but it was also the sign of a deep thinker, someone heavy with wisdom. It was not looked upon as a negative state. The melancholic brooded, mulled things over, recognized that they were a tiny, lonely figure on a vast ocean canvas, the heavy weather looming above, about to be tipped whole into the sea's open chest.

Surfing can become more than riding the wave. It can be experienced as immersion in big nature, in the aching silence of the sea suddenly punctuated by a cluster of breaking waves – a depression followed by urgent, perhaps anxious activity. Then, a big space opens up, and again there is deep calm. This time, maybe, it is a melancholic calm, but it is contemplative, not helpless, not powerless: it is not depression. If you indwell this experience, you allow your moods to be vanquished by the bigger moods of sea and sky.

The equation is straightforward (kind of): low pressure = surf = physical exercise + mindfulness = better health and positive attention to the environment. Therefore depression becomes melancholia or thoughtful existence, which means less need for antidepressants = less trace of antidepressants in the water = the green and blue gyms live forever.

Navigating the
Seasons

As surfers we become intuitive weather forecasters. And navigating the changing seasons (from wet and dry in the tropics to the four flavours of a year in the temperate climates) provides a constant lesson in mindfulness.

A piece of seaweed hung outside, checked each day for its moisture level, is an excellent natural barometer. Bladderwrack – found globally – is best. Dampish and swollen means rain on the way; dry and shrivelled means warm weather.

Surfers themselves can become like seaweed as they age, able to gauge weather changes, humidity levels and pressures from their own bodily sensations.

We can call this a form of bodymindfulness. Your whole being becomes attuned to pressure changes. Or, the world and its weather is tuning you. The vesicles or 'bladders' allow the seaweed to float just as your air-filled lungs allow you to; and the 'wrack' means 'wreck', or washed up on the shore, which is hopefully the end result of every surf! Alternative therapists claim a range of benefits from bladderwrack, too, including its use as a source of iodine, which is absorbed by the thyroid to make hormones.

WITH THE MIND OF WATER

Just as bladderwrack can be both a literal and metaphorical supplement to bodymindfulness, so we can think of the body of water in which we surf as an embracing body and mind, manipulating us physically as it is also 'thinking' us into being with its expressive moods. For me, a surfer whose home is the UK, these moods include cold snaps, howling gales and calm, relatively hot summers. As much as tropical and subtropical zones can have great surf with bath-warm water, they have climates rather than seasons.

The varied seasons, stitching into each other, teach you how to adapt. In fact, in my home in West Cornwall (where you can see the weather mustering its forces on the horizon) when people ask: 'What will the weather be like?' we reply 'Wait five minutes!' Weather changes can be rapid – sudden downpours, winds whipping up from nowhere, and then sun bursting through unexpectedly on an otherwise overcast evening for a blinding sunset. With the sea and weather thinking us into being in such a multitude of forms, who could ever get bored?

The changing seasons and daily gearshifts are absorbed and caught in the sea's skin – its colours, folds, tensions and moods. As surfers, we can learn to see into the future, scanning the horizon for signs of swell and gathering weather; checking the whitewater around headlands; looking for tracks of scudding seaskin indicating rips and currents; noticing colour changes along the coast caused by levels of sand movement; judging how beach contours are shaping up and where waves might break; and spotting the fresh whitecaps that tell of a shift in wind direction.

SEAL SKIN

Sailors and fishermen around the world have scores of terms to describe sea shapes, colours, and phenomena such as forms of fog, from thin 'sea frets' to cotton-wool-like 'rolls' sitting on the horizon and 'driving' mists in stiff winds. Another captive of the sea, the surfer knows too what's going on – the state of the tide, the size of the swell, the incoming weather – and by the art of bodymindfulness, in the blink of an eye, a whole host of factors come to bear upon the trained senses, and a pattern is registered.

Does the seal reflect on the fact that it swims in and under water? No – it swims, in total harmony with its surroundings. In every sense, it is in its element. For the bodymindful surfer, judgement of nature's panorama is not technical, instrumental, a matter of mere fact-finding. It is aesthetic, appreciative. Taking in your surroundings, often with little more than a glimpse, requires the glance of the connoisseur, the sea dog infused with the same spirit as the gnarly bladderwrack: a part of nature, looking around; not apart from nature, looking in. In your element.

So, when you put on your seal skin and enter the surf, strapping on the weather, allow yourself to become one with it, absorbed and absorbing, bodymindful. Educate your attention.

You are in your seal skin, slipping effortlessly below the silver water, navigating the now.

The Art
of the
Noseride

A classic meditation technique is to focus your attention on just one thing, to know it deeply. In longboard surfing, noseriding is considered the ultimate – and the sweetest – 'one thing'. To stand as if weightless at the very tip of the board, with a full 2 metres (9 feet) or more behind you, is to defy gravity; yet it is achieved by gravity because it works only by the compensating weight of water rushing over the back of the board so that you glide as if on a seesaw at the point of balance.

You travel by foot, step over step, to reach the nose, curling five toes over the front; and then maybe the other five, so ten toes embrace the tip and your back is slightly arched. This is the doorway to the soul of longboarding.

By comparison, riding just a short distance back from the nose in a 'stretch five' can feel heavy, ponderous, and prickly. The difference, when revealed, is startling. A 'clean' noseride seems both effortless and given, while a 'stretch five' stinks of effort.

The noseride must engage both vigilant and paradoxical attention. Vigilant attention is close noticing, attention to detail, and adjustment in ever-decreasing circles until a point of attention appears that shouts 'clarity!'. This is the mynah bird in Aldous Huxley's *Island*, set in a utopian Buddhist community on a Pacific island. It screams 'attention!' when people's minds wander or they forget the moment. The mynah bird is the monitor for a kind of acute attention that is a gaze rather than a glance.

A distinct point of balance in mind is necessary for footwork that leads to one or two feet placed over the tip of the board. Think outside the sphere of that point of balance and your steps become confused by the board rocking or sinking. This walk is one of extreme care – not on eggshells, but firmly, with the lightest of effort.

Just as important as vigilant attention is paradoxical attention – awareness of the big picture, taken in at a glance. If vigilant attention is the foreground of the gestalt, then paradoxical attention embraces the background. Together they encompass the whole picture, from wave movement, washing water, rail-to-rail turbulence, the will to motion and the tightness of muscle, the elegant lift in weight that comprehends how the tail of the board is getting locked in the wave face, just as the tip is rising slightly to allow a seesaw to form.

MOMENT OF GRACE

Mindful noseriding both attracts and resists practice at the same time. There is no question that practice, and associated vigilant attention, pays benefits; but you can also take your foot off the accelerator of practice and find that a genuine noseride emerges from nowhere because paradoxical attention has locked in. This is not luck, but a moment of grace. Seize that moment.

Mindfulness is then a holistic process that occurs as a unit: you notice your lack of footwork; that noticing itself is a result of mindfulness; and mindfulness is noticing things exactly as they are without distortion.

Noseriding is inevitably a passing moment embedded in the ever-present shifting moods of the sea and so cannot be claimed as an aspect of oneself. It was not 'you' who made the noseride and you cannot own it. So, actually, there is no point grabbing on to the noseride as that 'one thing' or of showing off when it happens because happiness cannot be found that way. At the heart of mindfulness is seeing the three Buddhist attributes of existence (in the Pali: *anicca*, *dukkha* and *anatta*; 'impermanence', 'suffering' and 'selflessness'), which are being in the moment, letting the moment pass, and then greeting the next moment without the intervention of conscious thought.

As you learn to noseride, you learn to integrate vigilant and paradoxical attention. Your experience melds and flows into one unfolding series of moments. Balance and footwork improves, as heavy stepping will only tip the board. Just like learning to integrate *anicca*, *dukkha* and *anatta* into your conscious life, when you accept that cross-stepping up and down the board is of equal importance to noseriding, it will happen without even thinking about it. At that point, effort seems to be effortlessly suspended, a doorway to the soul, and then a silence breaks in.

Here, the Buddha hangs ten.

The Craft
of the
Tuberide

The tuberide is the template for a hundred stories and a formative experience for the soul. While the noseride can be *anicca*, *dukkha* and *anatta*, riding the tube plunges you into a moment of *samskara* – a rapidly unfolding series of impressions that lock in memory as a 'formation' that can forever be recalled and retold.

It is a rinse in nature, a pure moment of 'given' mindfulness. Nature's body at its most elegant and geometric demands adaptation to the moment and leaves an indelible mark on the surfer's bodymind. It may only be a fleeting moment of joy but it's one you'll never forget – a moment of expansive connection, wrapped and then unwrapped in saltwater.

SHAPE-SHIFITNG

The tube is open to any surfer on any piece of equipment. Heavy tubes break over razor sharp reefs in shallow water, inviting unwanted natural tattoos in the form of scars. Lighter tubes build at point breaks over pebble bottoms, or beach breaks over sand, combed by offshore winds.

The key to tubes is 'shaping'. Shaping is central to surfing – boards are shaped by shapers and elegant surfing is all about adjusting to the contours of the wave. Shaping in tuberiding is about fitting the body and board to ride just behind the falling curtain.

To the untrained eye, the surfer inside the tube is apparently doing nothing. But this laconic 'doing nothing' is precisely the aim, and despite appearances it is the result of a huge amount of practice, preparation, timing, experience and knowledge.

At such moments you are at one with the wave both physically and mentally, intently relaxing. However, it is also at the most extreme moment of danger (perhaps you are over a section of poisonous fire coral) when you need to empty your mind in the void of the tube. The heavy-duty yang of the wave's spin from crest to trough, combined with the delicate yin of space and the unexpected emergence of opportunity is where the Taoist principle of *wu wei* ('non-action', 'non-doing') is manifest.

One of the central themes in Taoism is not acting until the conditions and timing are right. Acting at the right time, and not overreacting, is the essence of tuberiding. In fact, Taoism believes that, until the time is right, nothing will happen anyway, so a large part of *wu wei* is maintaining connection with the universal flow of the Tao. When it becomes clear that the time has arrived, only then do you act, by doing nothing.

The idea of action/non-action is that, instead of attaching your conscious will to a desired outcome, you maintain a willingness for your preferred outcome to arise, but do not cling to any specific end result. You can then allow the deeper motivations and conditions for your actions (not your personal agenda or ego) to bring about the actual, unfolding occurrence.

Action has two facets: the first is that you're going to take action – take off on a wave and get tubed without the fast-descending curtain taking you out. However, to emerge from the tube, non-action is also essential. Inside the tube, there should be no sense of internal resistance – keep your eyes open, stay low, aim for the exit, reacting only when the wave demands. It's very easy to overreact. By staying low and 'doing nothing' you embody non-action.

FINDING YOUR CENTRE

It is likely that successful tuberides are achieved by a person well-practised in hollow waves. But riding the tube is not just about skill. To ride the tube you need to have found a centre of peace or emptiness within yourself – something beyond 'me, myself and I'. The Tao doctrine of non-action within action and riding the tube require an immense amount of personal courage as you give up your sense of control. You have to be able to admit that you do not know what is next. So, by truly embodying the principle of *wu wei*, tuberiding becomes the ultimate craft, a part of crafting the soul.

If you are in a complete state of emptiness and do something deriving from that state, with no intrinsic planning or motivation behind it, then there is no ego. You are connected to the flow of the universe that is moving inside you, and you emerge from the fast-moving tuberide, grinning from ear to ear.

Tao's the time.

Breath
of Water

One of the most common problems when learning to surf is the tendency to panic and stop breathing calmly, just when you need a fluent rhythm of inhalation and exhalation. It is caused by the anxiety of the wipeout. But one of the basic techniques of meditation, and of mindfulness, is to follow the breath, using it as a focus for staying in the moment. All very well when seated on a cushion, but how to be mindful and follow the breath when it is pressed out of shape amid the (understandably) mild panic of our first attempts to stand on the board?

Following the perspective that surfing as mindfulness is not 'in' you but in your connection to the world around you, a good tip for learners is to forget about following your breath and instead follow the 'breathing' of the wave. This is easier said than done, but attending to the breath of the wave is liberating. The wave's inhalation is the rising blue-green face, exhaling as it breaks into churning whitewater. The unbroken wave holds the air like an expanding lung, while the breaking whitewater releases the air in a gasp, from the sigh of a small wave to the consuming, mega bellows of big waves.

As you follow the peak before it breaks, you will be truly surfing the 'curl', the fastest and most critical point of the wave, if only for seconds. Here, you will be propelled by the engine room of the wave's expanded lung, before the breath expires in a mass of foam. And here, in the breath of water, you are invited to join its expression and find flow.

FINDING FLOW

The most stylish surfers have an abundance of flow. They do not hesitate, stutter or look as if they may fall at any moment. They follow from the held breath to the out-breath of the spinning ride in one continuous trajectory. Flow and style are intimately linked. The key to flow is to avoid turning inwards, committing your attention instead to incorporating obstacles presented by the wave into the ride. For example, a sudden liquid ledge popping up on the wave's face is used like a skateboard ramp to gain a little speed; a collapsing section provides a good opportunity to float over it and accelerate rather than allow it to flip your rail and send you tumbling.

The movement of attention from your own heroic performance to whatever the wave throws at you is collaborative expertise. Here, you don't master a skill, you incorporate it through adaptation. For surfers, moving from supposedly heroic individualism as your locus of control to collaborative expertise involves a developing awareness of how your surfboard, the wave patterns, and other surfers in the water help or hinder your flow. The peak of blue-mindful activity in surfing embraces an extended cognition – moving out of your personal consciousness 'cage' to immerse yourself in the ever-changing elements of board design, wave types, and crowd behaviour.

The paradox of this shift from 'inside cognition' as the locus of expertise to 'extended cognition' is that mastery can be gained much more quickly than the well-known 10,000 hours rule of 'Practice! Practice! Practice!' This is because the world around you is achieving a lot of the mastery on your behalf. Your 'skill' is to attend deeply to this process by becoming a part of it. Let the wave do its work. When the lip tubes over you, take a seat in the 'green room' and enjoy the view.

The centre of balance for expertise is shifted from mastery to adaptation and cooperation, where the strain of ego responsibility is lifted. But don't necessarily rid yourself of it. Of course, control, focus and attention is needed from the individual, but this is embedded in what the environment affords. Isn't this what we mean by 'letting go'? It is not giving up or denying responsibility; it is, rather, the ability to respond.

Mindful behaviour, as the Buddha's teaching shows, is first and foremost a 'letting go' and not a 'taking on responsibility'. Thinking for others is not mindful. So, try not to think on the wave's behalf as you adapt; try not to outwit the crowd or transfer your own limitations on to the design of the board. Embrace board, wave and crowd. Care for, and with, the wave's trajectory and personality. Shift the locus of expertise from self to extended world. There's a simple guideline: when mindfulness practitioners say 'breathe', remember where the air comes from. Follow its flow. Watch the wave. Stick with it and to it.

Inspired by
Nature

Many moons ago on a surf trip to East Africa, sitting outback, I saw a tiger-shark fin rising from the water. Red sulphur rushed through me, turning black and cold inside. When I met the eye of the shark a penetrating stare scorched my nerves. In the stark clarity of shock, I realised that if we were not exchanging gazes, I might already be in the throes of an attack.

Perhaps the shark would not have shown itself unless it was curious. Fear gave way to a rush of relief, though my nerves were fried and my gut had turned to tar. Twelve feet of carnivore slipped beneath the surface, then moved gracefully away with the current. My heart pounding, I was left with a peculiar sense of calm.

ANIMAL FAMILIAR

Surfers all over the world have stories of close encounters with sealife to tell. These intense experiences serve as reminders that, when we surf, we need to be fully grounded in our senses, especially when visiting new spots for the first time.

We must tune in to the immediacy of sea mammals, the flowing fish, the dipping seabird, the curious seal, the unfolding wave, as an invited guest, not an owner. An approaching creature can be seen as a visit from a host or an animal familiar. In shamanism (a spiritual practice found in cultures around the world from ancient times to today) familiarity does not breed contempt, but respect.

Close encounters with sharks, seals and whales will certainly heighten your senses. At these moments, the real bodymind, the enteric nervous system, is the locus for mindful thought; your thinking is done for you. And inspiration from such moments is at the heart of biomimicry.

MIMICRY & MIMESIS

It could be said that biomimicry – design inspired by biological entities and processes – is fundamentally a form of mindfulness. It is the tangible result of a meditation upon nature, resulting in beautiful artefacts made through natural mirroring. Surfers have long used biomimicry to develop surfing equipment inspired by sea creatures. These include surfboard fins influenced by the dorsal fins of dolphins and wetsuits like seal skins.

Biomimicry demands that we begin by closely studying our natural environment. We can learn about more than just design by looking at sealife. The sea turtle is a great example. Sea turtles have existed for more than 100 million years; they are unrivalled ocean travellers, swimming over epic distances. Green sea turtles can stay under water for five hours, slowing their heart rate to as little as one beat every nine minutes to conserve oxygen. This provides a lesson in mindfulness – imagine what it is like to breathe as slowly as a sea turtle. Now push this one stage further and imagine the 'thought processes' of rocks – so slow as to be unimaginable to us frantic humans.

There are also powerful lessons to be learned from sealife about adaptation to circumstance. We humans often work against currents and winds, powering machines to journey in straight lines. This is hugely inefficient. Sea turtles drift along the current to travel. Mindfulness entails working with the given flow. Lao Tzu said: 'Conquering others takes force, conquering yourself is true strength.' We can expand this: conquering yourself is good; learning to respond and collaborate with others and our environment brings a shared strength beyond illusory divisions of self and other, humankind and nature. Biomimicry is such collaboration in action.

MINDFULNESS FOR THE PLANET

Sea turtles are one of the few animals to eat sea grass. A radical decline in sea-grass beds (perhaps from coastal development or climate change) would lead to fewer sea turtles. Beach dunes are highly dependent on sea turtles' eggs, which provide nutrients for dune vegetation; strong dune root systems help retain the sand and protect beaches from erosion. The threat of beach erosion is a threat to the quality of breaking waves at beaches, which need healthy supplies of sand to dissipate incoming wave energy and deliver smooth peeling rides, cherished by surfers around the world.

We started out looking at sealife to design better boards. We arrive at a timeless truth: all living things are interconnected and interdependent. All life is linked to water and the creatures that live within it. The more we educate ourselves about sealife and the issues facing this ecosystem, the more we will want to help ensure its health and to cultivate mindfulness on behalf of the planet by tending the oceans.

Hubris &
Humility

Surfing offers an uplifting spiritual rinse. But the same 'great mind' that raises you up can just as readily humble you with serious injury. The highs of surfing come pretty regularly and that's why surfers continue going back for more. The significant highs are those that are 'deep': they are achieved when an event deepens into an experience. Indeed, we could define mindfulness, where it is an eco-logical identification rather than an ego-logical inflation, as the activity that turns a potentially passing event into a long-lasting experience.

Deep highs are different from ego-driven inflations. Surfers who like to show off, strutting their stuff without regard for others and without helping the less able, may suffer from what the ancient Greeks called hubris or excessive pride. Icarus flew too close to the sun and suffered a fall. Some may show off in front of others they deem lesser than themselves, but perhaps punishment from the great mind in the form of a wipeout awaits them.

Talented surfers could guide others rather than behave pompously, and many do act brilliantly as mentors and role models. In surfing, as in life, the mindful approach is one of inclusion, where everyone is encouraged to perform according to their capability, not some ideal imposed by a hierarchy.

But ultimately it is not fellow surfers who call out those who are inflated. It will be the sea that brings them down to earth, as the sun did in melting the wax that attached Icarus's wings. The sea is the great leveller as it is also, for surfers, the great mind that embraces our unique passions and absorbs us as we too are absorbed by the gifts and bruises that waveriding can bring.

NEMESIS AT THE DOOR

Injury at the hands of the sea is neither malevolent nor spiteful, it is just the great mind changing gears. It is frustrating to be out of the water through torn cartilage, hamstring, ligaments, or pulled muscles. But this does provide time for contemplation. And there is a form of hubris far worse than that of the grandstanding titan.

The injuries we have dealt the body of the sea are the sobering result of our collective hubris. Our polluting of the oceans, particularly with non-degradable plastics, has already been catastrophic. Thinking for all these years that we could get away with dumping waste and sewage beyond our coastlines, we are now suffering the consequences and must act quickly.

This is surely the greatest test of collective mindfulness facing humankind. Traditional mindfulness-as-meditation, if it exists only to benefit the individual, is a luxury; if its inherent connection to life beyond selfhood is taken seriously, then collaborative,

eco-logically mindful activity becomes a necessity.
Not as an add-on but as the natural progression of
mindful practice.

Our collective hubris has led to us flying too close
to the sun. Is there still time for us to avoid the fate
of Icarus?

WHAT THE WORLD AFFORDS

All serious surfers are natural ecologists – the sea
shapes you that way. We cannot afford to retreat into
contemplation. We must step into collective action.
In Buddhism, the Threefold Way – that builds towards
awakening through the progressive cultivation of ethics,
meditation and wisdom – can be described as joining
together ethical action, concentration and insight into
daily activity. This relates to the 'three jewels' – Buddha
as teacher; Dharma as the knowledge contained in the
teachings; and Sangha as the supportive community.

As we develop our spirit of ecological awareness
and convert it into determined action, we can think

of the Buddha in terms of the ocean-as-teacher; Dharma as the blue mindfulness not 'in' us, but in what the ocean affords; and Sangha as all who participate in the ocean, including ourselves as surfers.

The world is telling us that it needs urgent attention due to our hubris. As Gaia, it is a living organism of which we are a part but from which we have come apart in mindlessness. We need to reshape our lifestyles, grounded in humility.

The surfing industry, for years a polluter through the use of petrochemical-based surfboards and wetsuits, has woken up to change and has begun sourcing sustainable materials. But this effort must be rapidly accelerated. It has taken too many generations to come to the realization that the so-called 'developed' world (based on neoliberal, capitalist modes of aspiration and acquisition) is ruining the planet we call home. Not collectively thinking through reparation in the next few generations is unthinkable. Let's shift from today's ego-logy to a future, mindful eco-logy.

Sound
Healing

Put your head underwater while a pod of dolphins
is playing around you and you might hear a marvellous
orchestrated series of 'clicks' as the dolphins converse –
socializing, maybe telling jokes or singing saltwater
songs. The clicks are not dull, but bright, sonorous
and musical.

The coming together of sound and surfing is another
dimension of the mindful experiences the sea affords.
Nature offers a rich soundscape – the sucking, crashing
and splashing of waves, the whistling and howling of
winds, the rattle of rain against the drumhead of the
water, distant thunder, birds cawing, the smack of a
diving gannet as it pierces the sea's skin.

Surfing adds its own counterpoint – the bottom turn sends a salt spray over the back of the wave and produces an audible skidding sound; slipping into a big tube produces a cavernous echo as the lip plunges; wiping out smacks the surface. One of waveriding's most delicious realizations is that you not only have a front seat at this natural concert: you are a welcome part of the orchestra.

A good analogy is the surfer-as-drummer. Your part is to stay, like a drummer, with the tempo of the wave. Drummers can play just ahead or just behind the beat to create syncopation, a feeling that the music is elastic. Aiming for elasticity, oily waters underfoot, wind stripping foam from the wave's lip, you glide, bending the cutback so hard that your fins pop clear in a sharp wail, snapping back as the wave collapses whole. You kick out in an arc, allowing you to snatch the board in mid-air and land with grace. Paddling out again, your gaze is already anticipating and summarizing the coming set wave. This song-line is pure joy. Running underneath is the bigger beat of wave motion: gathering; rearing up; crashing down in a dead beat. And then da capo. Surfing is circular music.

CONCERT IN THE SEA

It may seem like a strange suggestion that surfers perform not just to the music of the sea, but to recorded music through waterproof headphones. Yet when we explore the coming together of surfing and music, we unlock new experiences where waveriding feels wonderfully playful and unselfconscious. Music can give surfing a lift, zip, angle, or element of surprise: rich, frantic, soulful, hard-driving, open, graceful, fluid, cool or lyrical. This is surfing with music's prescription.

Let's try surfing to a jazz track for longboarders. Your first reaction as the music kicks in might be to find a balance where you can hear the music and sea simultaneously. Sounds will mix – swell moving, wave cracking, lips smacking on the drumhead of the water, then – in the headphones – horns and piano start up.

Set approaching. You paddle. But this time, you are not just responding to the wave, you are also responding to the music in your ear. So you arc a bottom turn, stall, cross-step, and hang under the lip. The music influences your footwork, weighting and unweighting the board to create trim. At times you may be uncoordinated as the beat is syncopated, your rhythm a series of missteps. This adds to the challenge. Just try riding in a straight line: do less – the lyrical, minimal tone of a solo against the drummer's brushwork. Actually, the meshing of the movement of the wave with quick feet and bright music offers the potential weaving of many points of balance.

Why not repeat the experiment with different kinds of music and compare notes with friends? Is this against the grain of mindful surfing, or does this open a door to a contemporary experience of mindfulness? If dance and ballet are performed to music, why not set surfing ablaze to music, not after-the-fact (like a film soundtrack) but live, red hot, during the session?

BLUE NOTE

Bringing together water, board, body and music affords
a unique form of blue mindfulness that can expand
the senses: a fusion of dance with hanging blue notes
of the jazz trumpeter (slightly acid, a little brittle).

In jazz, the flattened blue note is intentionally
imperfect. Its soupçon of sour distortion is just enough
to give the note flavour. It needs the gentle squash
and bitterness to bring out the 'blue' of the bruise. So
the blue mindful moment is achieved. Mindfulness
in surfing can be an experience of ocean-born sound,
with the added injection of pre-recorded blue notes.

Or find your own aesthetic: Afrobeat, jive, funk,
punk, pop, a waltz or a stomp.

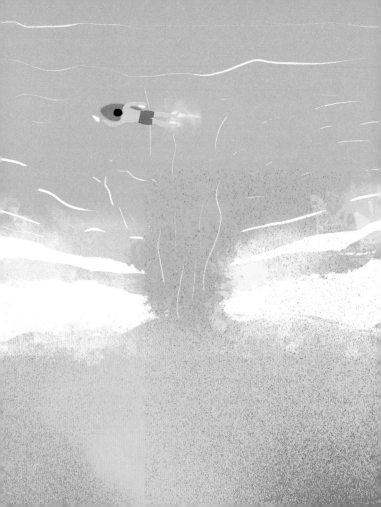

Simplicity

Every now and then it's good to abandon the board and swim out for a bodysurf, stripping back to find greater simplicity. No carving cutbacks, no noserides, just straight lines, skin on water. Even in a wetsuit, closer to the surface of the wave you can really feel the suck of gravity on take-off, the stretched tension from the bottom to the top of the drop.

Bodysurfing is 'close' mindfulness, skin on skin. It leaves near-invisible tracks, milky inscriptions on the water that fade in an instant. Slip under the duvet of the unfolding water into the empty bed of a barrel, all noise cancelled; wake up at the shoreline, memories stained indigo with sea inks.

The sensation of seawater on skin brings the body into focus in a way that walking through air does not. We become sealife. Surfboards can sometimes be a thin layer of separation from our medium, perhaps limiting our complete immersion in and identification with this liquid flux. Bodysurfing helps us slip into the ocean and relax amid supporting sealife. The mindful moment comes when you feel part of the ocean, without working against it. Your body of contemplation becomes transparent, sea-through. Then as you slip out of a tuberide under a rising moon, your inner fires will be stoked.

All this talk of stripping back the tools of waveriding may not inspire you to abandon hard-railed surfboards for bodysurfing permanently. But trying a variety of surf craft and approaches is certainly key for avoiding mundane repetition and the rut of doing just one thing. The thin wooden bellyboard is another great tool to try, and acts as a humble, elegant bridge between the surfboard and pure, board-free bodysurfing. There is a long and rich history of bellyboarding on locally felled woods around the world, from the 'palangs' of Papua New Guinea to the 'alaias' of Hawaii and 'itako-nori' boards of Japan.

LEARNING TO SPEAK H$_2$O

The simplicity of bodysurfing can help our minds learn the vocabulary of the sea, and we can apply this across our wider surfing lives. The language of rips and currents is extremely useful to learn (rips funnel tide and wave energy back to the deep sea). They will get you beyond the whitewater with ease, but appreciating their hazards is as important as discovering their uses. A strong rip can pull you far out, and being caught in this while swimming can be frightening – you lose energy if you battle against the rip. It can overwhelm you.

Dealing with such a current requires mindfulness. You have to shut down the panic mode and relax (not easy) to conserve energy. Let your body be like a jellyfish; concentrate. Then, swim slowly but purposefully at right angles to the movement. Rips are normally quite narrow and do not pull you under, as they operate in surface water only. They are like shallow rivers running out to sea. Soon you will clear the current and be in calm water.

Rips are blessings in disguise – highways that take traffic but also attract accidents. The best way to converse with rips is to learn by immersion – but first, spot the currents from the beach, work out how they are running in relation to the breaking waves, then plan your geometries. Know where you must take a 90-degree turn, visualize this and take the mental map out with you. Most importantly, watch those who are already mindful – experienced surfers, old salts, the bodysurfers. They are your guides to the glide.

CURRENTS UNDER THE SKIN

Pain is a universal human experience. Kids and teenagers get 'growing pains' in their legs at night. As we grow older, our acquaintance with pain only becomes more intimate.

Can we learn the language of our own inner currents and tides? Can we smooth the jagged, confused hubbub of pain sensations by bringing *karuna* into the conversation? In the Buddhist world, *karuna* means 'compassion'. We can adopt this compassion towards our aches and pains and, with a technique we could call 'body surfing', we can choose not to ignore them – we imagine a wave of attention flowing over the entire body. Starting at the feet, move up and inside the body – notice temperature, weight and feeling. Accept, include, relax with all your experience. Calm, rest and sleep will follow. This 'bodysurfing body scan' can be used at any time to reduce discomfort and anxiety.

The simplicity of bodysurfing – in both its forms – puts us directly in touch with experience. We become more sensitive to our body and its rhythms. And on the wave, we get in touch with nature's body as a whole. Compassionate attention provides a gateway and a path to *karuna* that is expressed in caring action towards those environments existing within and around ourselves.

The Soul
of Surfing

There are tens of millions of surfers in the world – a rainbow nation of all ages and backgrounds, all seeking the fulfilment of waveriding. You can surf reefs, points, beach breaks, river bores and inland wavepools. Surfing is used to promote gender equality and other aspects of social justice. Adapted surfboards allow the physically challenged to surf. Surfing is now a common therapy for mental ill-health and recovery from conditions such as post-traumatic stress disorder. Surfers have been among the most effective groups within environmental activism and education. Surfers may seek hollow waves but, whatever else it may be, surfing is anything but hollow – it is packed with possibility.

For many, the definition of the 'soul of surfing' will simply be 'the pure love of water breaking', fulfilled through a range of equipment and approaches. From an adaptive surfer with cerebral palsy riding in a specially developed surf seat with friends, to someone so skilled on a board that they know the inner workings of the tube, where time stands still and pure spirit distils from the cure of saltwater all around.

For some, soul surfing is attentive collaboration with the environment, with sea creatures, wearing the seal skin, rising up and down with the tideline, celebrating the salt-stain. Or, to be more inclusive in an ever-growing world of riding river bores and inland wavepools, soul surfing is an active dance in a water-cloak.

Whatever your definition, the soul of surfing is a lure, a beneficent addiction. The minute you finish a session and drain your sinuses, you cannot wait to get in the water again. It becomes your natural habitat. And even when you've suffered a trauma at its hands, the urge to heal the trauma through surfing is irresistible.

ARETE

Reflecting the emerging countercultural youth movement of the time, the term 'soul surfer' appeared in the 1960s and blossomed in the 1970s. It described the non-commercial, non-competitive surfer who rode waves for pure joy. Theirs was a more spiritual pursuit. The term stood in opposition to the rise of professional surfing, paralleled later in freeride snowboarding that developed as a loose but electric off-piste response to the rigid rules of ski competition.

This is arguably a more selfish journey, riding only for the personal gain of pleasure. But this approach framed surfing as art, dance and performance as opposed to sport. Yet it was misleading to polarize surfing this way, implying professional surfers could not be soul surfers. International competitors may well experience as much of the soul of surfing as those teaching kids to stand up on a board for the very first time.

The ancient Greeks developed competitive sport as a complex cultural, ritual activity, birthing the Olympic

Games. Sport was a way of saying something through the body, a form of persuasion or rhetoric in front of an audience, as well as an aesthetic display of beauty. The Greek notion of *arete* ('excellence' and virtue of any kind) is demonstrated through an activity that is mastered to its core, so that its soul, its highest perfection and challenge is known and shown. Surfing's total reliance on unpredictable ocean conditions separates it from other sports. Yet surfing, even at the highest level of competition, remains an aesthetic display. And equally, even as beginners, surfers are, in a sense, competitors; we must meet the challenge of the ocean, attempting to do better, go further, than yesterday.

CELTIC TRIQUETRA

Surfing stitches together body, heart, mind, community and sealife. Surfing is also strenuous (with highs and lows like the tide) and so requires love, courage and devotion – the three gifts of the heart (think Tristan and Iseult, Richard the Lionheart, Saint Augustine).

In Celtic art there is the triquetra (the trinity knot): a single strand that appears to be three links forming a knot. Cut at any point and the three-way symmetry is lost. Snip any part and the whole unfolds. This knot is a potent symbol for mindfulness: the bringing together of heart, mind and body into an indivisible entity – the soul. Blue mindfulness maintains attention, retaining the integrity of this knot. The soul of surfing rests in the courage and will to bring the entity about. It is an initiation, the revealed mystery of awe and humility in the face of the sea.

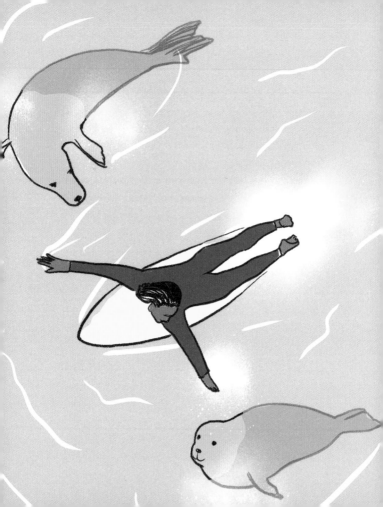

The Gift of
Hospitality

Every surfer craves the experience of surfing with dolphins, the companionship of seals, or sitting close to basking sharks (not too close – though the sharks are harmless, getting caught by a swishing tail will put you in real trouble). An encounter with such sealife offers an immediate connection with the animating soul of all living beings.

Even the wipeout offers hospitality, since it invites you into the depths of the water. It provides you a glimpse of blue mindfulness by inducing a mixture of elation and fear, as you skitter across the wave face before being swallowed whole, only to be reborn in an afterlife of spluttering survival. You emerge humbled,

schooled in deeper awareness, respectful, attentive
to the ocean as great leveller and venerable teacher.

NESTING IN THE WAVE

Through surfing we can, and must, learn a form of
mindfulness that is really a kind of awakened gratitude.
If we resist the rhythms and energies of our watery
surroundings, if we believe we are at war with the world,
we miss the truth that we are always and already in its
pocket, and we cannot hear the generous, unceasing
invitation to nest within it and learn its ways.

Nesting in a wave is not an invitation to see it as
property of your own. When you travel to surf (very
likely as you probably don't live on the tideline like
a limpet) be aware of your visitor status – you are
an outsider. You have not 'discovered' any surf break.
You are a guest of the sealife that calls it home. You
enter a circle of hospitality that should be honoured,
not broken. The host receives, the guest reciprocates
in kind – with kindness and respect.

The root of 'hospitality' and 'hospital' comes from the Latin *hospes*, meaning guest. And as a guest you can honour the hospitality offered with trustworthiness, tolerance of difference, and awareness that there is much to be learned through abandoning one's own cultural baggage (which might be packed with preconceptions and misconceptions about people and places).

Nesting in that wave, finding your gratitude, you can discover that blue mindfulness extends itself effortlessly to include values and practices that benefit the surfing community and its wider spirit.

SEEKING THE PRIZE THAT IS NOT LOST

Mindfulness is not usually the first topic that comes up in surf-related conversations. Perhaps that is down to a certain idea of what mindfulness is. But let's for a moment suspend the commonly understood idea of mindfulness as an occasional practice inserted into the daily routine.

Truth is, surfers do not necessarily need to take up this kind of mindfulness: the blue world of surfing is already a mindful experience waiting to be articulated, and every surfer can step into this world through a simple shift in perception: not 'I surf', but 'the ocean affords surfing'. This is the paradigm shift, and through it we become permanently mindful. Ending polluting behaviour, evolving activities such as sustainable surf tourism, and organizing bottom-up, community-centred wealth-sharing practices – these require no effort when the mind is blue and the spirit swims in open waters.

POIESIS

The Greek *poiesis* describes a craft that is elevated into an art. The word literally means 'to make' and is the root of the word 'poetry'. It implies that poetic creation moves beyond technical skill into connoisseurship and expertise. If there is a key to shifting from pedestrian or instrumental surfing to blue mindfulness, it may be found in the dedication needed to transform surfing into active poetry, into poetic statement. Such refinement leads the surfer towards greater heights of awakened gratitude – not only towards the ocean and its generosities, but towards surfing itself as a form, a history, a legacy that is the gift of centuries and pioneers past.

Like the fundamental techniques of poiesis in the Homeric epics – in which standard lines are repeated to give form and rhythm – so your slow mastery begins with repeated practice of the surfing fundamentals. You check conditions, prepare equipment, paddle out, duck-dive, take-off, pop-up, trim, kick-out, greet the mysteries, listen to the locals, take the surf on offer as a gift, exit with humility.

You are on your way to blue mindfulness. You are on your way to poetry.

Never
Too **Old**

You're never too old to surf. Only injury and physical infirmity will prevent you, as your mind will be much younger than your body. Your experiences of mindfulness (not in your body, but in the world) are timeless. Mindfulness in the world extends to etiquette – respecting and caring for others in the water. The surf community must foster accessibility for older surfers. As young surfers develop their skills at local breaks, older surfers will be able to educate them in the etiquette of surfing, sharing their wisdom in the waves.

Older surfers also model possibilities for the young, showing them that you can follow your dream into your seventies, maybe even into your nineties. At twenty, supple and taking on maximum risk, it is surely good to think you might be surfing for another fifty years or more, part of the environment's colour and form, full of folk tales.

If you have surfed for many decades and are still coming back for more, part of the continuing lure is that surfing is far from easy – it is as challenging as it is addictive. Moments of pure glide experienced on a wave are impossible to achieve on land. You have to grasp the three elements of the Celtic triquetra – moving body, moving body of water, moving body of the surfboard – and keep them interlinked.

The triquetra – a single strand that appears to be three links forming a knot – is a potent symbol for surfing and mindfulness: the bringing together of bodymind, saltwater and surfboard. Bliss is not guaranteed; wipeouts are frequent, but mindful moments are more clearly cherished as you get older.

Surfing does not just keep your body in shape; it continually works the mind and feelings. Telling 'old salt' tales is reminiscence therapy. Putting together a half-decent take-off, bottom-turn, trim, kick-out combination is, in large part, muscle memory. Mindfulness for the older surfer can become an aid in resisting mindlessness, keeping forgetfulness at arm's length as you slip into the routine of paddle, up to your feet in one continuous motion, and then tuck under the aquamarine curtain. As the pattern of neurons fires, so an activity performed thousands of times unfolds, but – and this is the mindful moment – it unfolds differently on every wave. Blue mindfulness in surfing is living, wide-eyed, in the midst of surprise.

GRACE IN THE WAVES

The wisdom of past generations has to be kept alive as surfing, still a relatively young activity for the global masses, deepens its history. Within that history, it is only relatively recently that a code of surfing etiquette has been formalized along Confucian lines and is based on grace – 'courteous good will'.

China's K'ung Fu-tzu, also known by his Latinized name of Confucius, believed that society could be improved if individuals behaved decently towards one another, guided by a formalized code. Democracies establish their codes via constituted rights and responsibilities that offer (at least in principle) equality of opportunity, social justice and the rule of law. Of course, nobody wants to police others with a rigid list of regulations, but caring for and respecting others in the water can be achieved with a few simple guidelines. Beginning with who has 'right of way' on a wave, where surfers never 'drop in' on another surfer (taking off on a wave in front of someone who is already up and riding, thereby threatening their safety with a collision).

With increasing crowds and the chance of collisions, frustration and aggression inevitably creep into some surfing breaks. Perhaps it's the passing of time that teaches people that sharing and giving away waves to others is rewarding. As young surfers develop their styles and skills at local breaks, older surfers can educate them in the mindful etiquette of the line-up (where you 'line up' and take turns to ride a wave). Such guidelines can shape a democracy of practice.

We can take our Confucianist code of conduct and translate it into a Tao: a way, a path, a route, that is both a right of way, and a rite of way (a way of doing the right thing as a mindful, ceremonial gesture). The Tao of safety and respect will teach you not to endanger others, for example, by not abandoning your board unless you are certain that there is no surfer or swimmer behind you. Respect breeds respect – listen to your elders who will almost certainly offer sound advice.

Zen
through Diversity

Zen as a state of mind is of 'no-mind' (*mushin* in Japanese and *wuxin* in Chinese). Meditators practise this mental state of 'no-mind' to achieve an open awareness unfettered by thought or emotion. We may think that only a few dedicated martial artists or Buddhist and Taoist monks could reach such states. However, Zen has always taught that awakening is a possibility open to all, a democratically available potential. In its principles, also, Zen recognizes neither hierarchy nor privilege.

The promise of Zen 'no-mind' through surfing is there for everyone. People of all shapes, sizes and backgrounds can ride waves and chase that promise.

The ocean is a blanket of democracy. Surfing can be a way of feeling strong, healthy and beautiful beyond the media's narrow imposition of body norms. The ocean welcomes everyone with a mind to rinse. And we can all embrace the soak of turbulent water, perhaps infecting others with the gift of stoke.

PINK NOSES

Mindfulness in surfing has given rise to extraordinary programs for inclusivity. A number of excellent surf schools from the Philippines to Mexico work with vulnerable young people at risk of, or diagnosed with, mental health issues, learning difficulties or physical disability. The visually impaired are taught to 'see otherwise', the deaf to 'hear otherwise' as their other senses become attuned.

Women have been breaking down social barriers through surfing from Bangladesh to Papua New Guinea for many years. Paddling out can be a way to shatter long-standing stereotypes, where the ocean is a place of liberation. At surf clubs in the patrilineal, patriarchal areas of Papua New Guinea, by painting the noses of half of all surfboards pink, female surfers are given exclusive ownership of boards and equal status is made visible. While not necessary in the matrilineal areas of the country, where it counts this simple tool promotes women's participation and gives greater recognition in the waves. The pink nose is a symbol of open values. Attitude precedes act, and there is no mindful act without an open attitude.

JOY WITHOUT LIMITS

More and more surf schools now use surfing to work with people who have suffered from traumatic life experiences, such as exposure to violence, poverty, isolation or bullying. Being in the water helps calm the mind. Surfing also promotes resilience, which is critical to long-term wellbeing. Getting wiped out and climbing back onto your board to do it again boosts self-esteem. There is an example of an eight-year-old girl with cerebral palsy and epilepsy who could not walk unaided. After surfing on specially adapted equipment, and with the support of instructors, she soon gained the confidence to start walking on land.

Adaptive surfing – which can accommodate amputees, quadriplegics and people with cerebral palsy – is one of the most inspiring aspects of surfing, bringing joy to thousands around the planet, with pioneering board designs, newly established world-title competitions and specialist magazines. The ocean provides a medium where physical limitations and mental barriers can be surmounted, more movement becomes possible and a deeper connection to nature is fostered. The sea can heal scars, and new equipment is starting to allow adaptive surfers to ride inside the barrel, where they too can share in the experience of time standing still.

Genuine mindfulness will not enable or maintain social discrimination. Mindfulness works on the basis of inclusivity and equality. It was not mindful to allow surfing to constellate around white youth culture in

1950s' California, especially as surfing was practised in ancient Hawaii as the sport of kings and queens. It was not mindful to ban black people from so-called 'whites-only' beaches in apartheid South Africa (where there is now a thriving black South African surf culture). It was not mindful to assume that kids with cerebral palsy couldn't be taken surfing. But we have now moved on through a mindful politics of democratic inclusion. Thus (for example) people who do not want to break with the dress codes of their religious faith or social tradition can now ride waves with appropriate modesty, in an ever-widening variety of adapted swimsuits, seasuits and hijabs.

Mindfulness is, again, more than a meditation technique. It is an artful being-in-the-world that deepens the momentary event into a transformative, transporting experience. It is qualitative, connective, leading simultaneously to inclusive acts of kindness and to those Zen moments that 'indwell' and fill the 'no mind' with riches.

Surfing
& Beauty

The arts are a wonderful vehicle for mindful being. They not only enrich our lives through pleasure, but also challenge us, prodding us to 'think otherwise'. There are many dimensions of art: the professional practitioner who has studied technique and history, and identifies with the label of 'artist'. And then there are the 'available' arts where each of us can choose our preferred medium and experiment.

Surfing can be described as a performance art – its professional elite engender awe at their polished presentations of ability and agility. For the majority of surfers, surfing is something more raw and crude, but is nevertheless filled with wonders all of its own.

Even at the beginner's level, surfing as a performance art and cultural activity goes beyond the functional and instrumental to embrace aesthetic qualities, affording grace and beauty. Most surfers feel the desire to perform, improve and perfect their skills with a certain degree of elegance and effortlessness.

Surfing can also develop a spiritual dimension. By maintaining connection with the water; building confidence; and bringing curiosity, passion and imagination to the party, you feel your senses begin to widen and your spirit dilate, no matter what your skills or physical abilities are or what other challenges you may face in everyday life. Every surfer, whatever their 'level', has felt the moment of stillness as you take off and fly towards shore. Time, in a paradox, stands still and a space of quietude emerges. Having tasted this precious fruit, you will no doubt want to taste it again and again through progressive stages as, with practice, your accomplishments and exquisite skills climb towards grace.

YOU CAN'T TEACH STYLE –
YOU HAD IT ALL ALONG

As surfers improve in ability, there is a transition from function to form. Experimentation begins to stretch the boundaries of the basic manoeuvres, as shortboarders go from the foundations of take-off, bottom-turn, top-turn and cutback, then into the air above the wave, even rotating twice with the board full-circle (at 720 degrees) and landing, still riding. The more elegant the manoeuvre, the bigger the pleasure in nailing it.

Longboarders, meanwhile, seek to walk the board with finesse, cross-stepping up to the nose and putting one or both sets of toes over the front tip for the sublime hang five or, better yet, hang ten. A radical version of the noseride is turning around to hang heels. Holding this manoeuvre through a tricky section is the high point of longboard expertise. Good stylists then cross-step back and possibly pull off a powerful drop-knee cutback, moving the board in the opposite direction to greet the unfolding wave's maximum point of speed.

Then turning back with this added momentum, perhaps to set up perfect trim and another noseride, rounded off with a clean kick-out to paddle back for more.

The longboard performance repertoire was first popularized as 'hotdogging' in 1950s' Californian surfing, though its origins can be traced to the Hawaiians who surfed giant boards in the 1930s at Waikiki, where the headstand was the classic manoeuvre – a yoga asana on a slippery, sliding mat!

A once popular event at surf contests was tandem riding, one surfer lifting their athletic, lightweight partner onto their shoulders while riding in. A permutation of this is the adult instructor who helps the young child build confidence by taking him or her on the front of their board – the child either rides prone or goes for the adventurous 'two standing' route.

Adaptive surfing allows physically challenged children and adults who cannot stand to surf to sit down on a custom-made board, with a helper steering from the back. All of these are 'available' performing arts and are a privilege to witness. Form and function fuse with balance and contemplation in an exhibition of blue mindfulness.

If the creative and mindful moment turns an ordinary event into an extraordinary experience, we can also say that the liquid world helps mould our body movements into performative expression.

The longboarder cross-steps to the nose. A performance atavism kicks in (deep in the memory of the brain) and ten toes curl over the tip. Without thinking, the back flexes in a 'soul-arch' and hands are held high. A performance 'imprint' – repeated across cultures and across the veil of time – flows out as you let go. The unfolding, timeless moment serves no purpose except to manifest the sublime. Merely form? Merely aesthetic expression? What a moment – of poise, contentment and harmony.

This is where style counts. And it turns out, all you need to learn it is the gift you already have. It was always already yours. Mindfulness will unlock it.

ACKNOWLEDGEMENTS

Thank you, with more than words can express, for all the love, inspiration, support and lessons in blue mindfulness from my wonderful family – Mum (Sue), Dad (Alan 'Fuz'), Lola and Ruben, Caity and Kara, my beautiful sisters Brioney and Phaedra, and brilliant nieces Izzy and Amelie. Thank you Planet Ocean and my cherished home surf break Gwenver. And above all thank you for all the shared waves of creative freedom with my gorgeous wife Sandy.